Anti-Mastery

Kate Maxwell

BookLeaf Publishing

India | USA | UK

Presentation by *BookLeaf Publishing*

Web: www.bookleafpub.com

E-mail: info@bookleafpub.com

ISBN: 9789360942274

First edition 2024

To all of the people who kept me swimming.

No sinking allowed.

ACKNOWLEDGEMENT

Thanks to my husband Pete, my sister Rachel and my bro-in-law Oliver, who helped me with the final push to get this done!

PREFACE

Inspired by my brilliant sister, Rachel Askew, who wrote 'How I Choose to Respond' last year, I joined this challenge to write something. Unfortunately, this challenge occurred during a turbulent period of house moving and shaking which prohibited me writing everyday. Instead, I have collected some random writings over the last 3 years. Notes in my phone when I have felt the need to write something. There is no theme. But it is reflection of me.

Rules

What I am finding
Most puzzling of all
Is that we humans
Have constructed
Our own
Rules for living.

Yet we have become
So bound by
These rules
That is starts
To feels like we are
'Being done to'
Rather than
'Doing it to ourselves'.

Rules can be changed.

So when I see
People being awkward
'According to the rules'
That sees people
Suffering in their lives,
It makes me angry.

It feels like really,
People
Cannot
Be bothered.

17/08/2020

I Feel Despair

I feel despair
That we are heading
In the wrong direction.
We've moved from centre
To extreme opposites
In a few short years.

People don't have enough.

What they have
Has been worked hard for
So they begrudge
Giving people
With less
More for nothing.

To the point where
People have been arguing
Against feeding children.

Poverty
Is a terrible thing.

Headaches
And heartaches

And whole body aches.

What does it mean
To be British these days?

It probably depends
Upon which area
Of the country
You live.

I've never felt
So disconnected from
The rest of the world.

29/10/2020

The Only Place in the World

5

"I feel like Richmond
Is the only place in the
World" my son told me.

31/12/2020

Senses

6

The birdsong
Mixed with
A gentle rustling
From the branches
Overhead
Thrummed in my ears
As I snaked
My way
Through the grass
Up to my knees.

07/06/2021

Get the Job

Get the job
Get the car
Run miles away and never look back.

Again again again
Keep your head.

When they leave,
Don't look back.

Hearts bursting
Wheels turning
Scorching sun and green grass
The bluest sky of my life.

Keep my head.

Rising stars
Constellations showing up
Everywhere.

Blue lights.
Breathe
Breathe
He's here.

Get a house
She's here
But she's gone.

New era
Keep your head.

Take my essence
Pour it away
Take her with it.
Gone.
Never forgotten.

Lost my head.

Fight
Fight
No fight.

There but
Not there.

Holding onto
New beginnings.

Prisms refracting
Colours
All around.

But I am grey.

Peace.

Silvers of light.

Nuchal cord
Won't stop us now.

Grey and blue.
Dashes of yellow.

Motionless.

29/04/2022

Pearl

Inside of me
There is a pearl.

Sometimes the pearl
Shines.

And feels steady
And good.

Other times
The pearl shakes
And quivers.

It starts
To vibrate.

I try to
Contain it
And stop it.

But that
Never works.

06/07/2022

The Pit

I can barely bring
Myself
To hope.

That life will ever
Feel mine again.

I fail
Everyone
Around me.

I should die.

But I can't.

For the one that
Feeds from
My breast
And cannot
Drink cows milk.

I will look
For something.

To pull

Me out.

But I fear
I am
Too far in.

20/02/2023

Dolce Far Niente

13

The Sweetness
Of doing
Nothing.

Ruin
Is the road
To transformation.

21/05/2023

Fright

Things that used to scare me:

Small spaces
Dying
Being buried alive

Things that scare me now:

Losing my children
Working full-time
Never being enough.

27/07/2023

New Obessions

15

A new obsession
With calf muscles

Three circular indentations
To the outer leg
In the shape
Of a triangle
And one
On the ankle joint.

Brown,
Toned,
Veined
And hairy.

Smooth
And muscly.

Pale, smooth
And chunky.

Slender to the ankle.

27/07/2023

3:54am

It's 3:54am.

Toilet and thirst.

The central
Table leaf.
Panic.
Where is it?

Racing thoughts.

House
House
House.

Tables.

12/11/2023

Waiting

I'm
Still
Waiting
For my life to start.

17/11/2023

The Floor

It's like the floor has dropped away
 And I am in free fall.
It is a bit floaty
But totally unnerving and unsafe.
My thoughts are loose and emotionless.
Vacant is the way
To keep something resembling ok.

I see the green light
In the corner of the room
Emanating from the emergency lighting.
It is where I anchor my vision
So I can keep moving my limbs
As the Pilates instructors voice fades in and out.

Suspension of time
And I am starting
To feel a flow.

The class ends too soon.
I realise the instructor
Is addressing me
Wants to remind me
To text her dates.
I put on my best smile

And tell her I will.

I turn away
Pretend to concentrate
Really hard
On putting my shoes on
And tying the laces.

I don't want anyone else to speak to me.

Someone does speak to me
And I can feel the mask
Coming down
Over my face
To squeeze out a friendly smile
And slip into the role
Of a normal person
For a few seconds.

We exchange pleasantries
About a person in common.
I try to sound jolly
Even though I feel nothing.

I have a sharp pain in my left side.
It is nothing to worry about.
But it is annoying
And I wish it would go away
Because it means I am forced

To acknowledge a feeling.
Then the other feelings
I am repressing
Try to fight their way out.

23/11/2023

Vegan Sausage Roll Shame

I'm eating.
A vegan sausage roll
In my dining room.

And I've decided
Not to close the curtain
Between me
And the electricians
Who are busy
Wiring up my kitchen.

I am aware
Of the sound
Of me.
Eating.

I start wondering
If they think
I'm a fat pig.

For eating
A Greggs sausage roll
In the middle of the day.

It's lunchtime

But I still feel ashamed.

I'm writing this down
To let myself see
How ridiculous
This thought is
So I can release it
And stop the anxiety
From
Surging
Through
My
Body.

24/11/2023

Earnest Eyes

Rushing
Swelling
Flooding my body.

Should I say yes?

I might put my head in the oven
Before I put a foot on the stage.

Earnest eyes
Expectation

Attention overload
For attention deficit.

Hiding in Plain Sight

08/12/2023

Deck the Halls

Deck the halls
With door handles
Curls of wood

Framing my delight
With silly
Jokes

Why do you have so many
Tools on your belt?

09/12/2023

Boxes of Books

Boxes of books
Keep giving me looks

Of despair

It's not fair!

We want to stand tall
On the shelves on your wall

Not in here

We're so near!

Next to the bookcase
Such an awful disgrace

Cast adrift

We are miffed!

I want to reach in
Grab a spine for the win -

I cannot.

Mind's to pot!

Swimming in murk
Lethargy lurks

Unwelcome.

Do some!

Put one on now
You lazy old cow!

I cannot.

Mind's to pot.

How long will we wait
For the particular date

Of our freedom?

To be gleesome!

14/12/2023

Anti-mastery

Anticipation
Of a smooth
Round
Shiny
Slightly charred
Shell

Smells
Like home

Warming
My hip
In my pocket.

Frustration.
Can't get in.
Soot
Builds up
Round my pink
Nails

Looks
Rotten.

Much like

My heart
Beneath my bones.

17/12/2023

Ode to a Window

You open up
The possibility
That this house might
Actually be
Ok.

Tea steaming as
I climb
The stairs, you bathe
Me in
Coral.

A waiting room
For things
Yet to find their
Final resting
Place.

An art gallery -
My delight.
A revolving door on
What was
Before.

The gap between

The life
I have and the
Life I
want.

Like walking through
the wardrobe
You aren't there
anymore for
Us.

Save for a
hairline crack
in our wall but
I feel
hopeful.

18/12/2023

Tired

I wish I could stop
This hurtling train.

But I'm
Tired.

Tired of pressing the brakes
Before it breaks.

Because it's gonna break
No matter what I try.

But I have to decide if
We all get broken
In the process.

Or if we can salvage
The good bits
Then move on.

18/12/2023

So Much Noise

In my head
Shed
In my head.

I am
The shed.

Sometimes
I'm dead.

Just an empty
Vessel.

Workman's
Trestle.

Other times

Chef's
Pestle.

A mighty
Castle.

I can't decide

Who to be.

Who is me?

Can I just be?

30/12/2023